ISBN 0 361 06278 8

Stories first published 1967.
Published 1984 by Purnell Books, Paulton, Bristol, BS18 5LQ, a member of the BPCC group.
Made and printed in Great Britain by Purnell and Sons (Book Production) Limited.
Phototypeset by Quadraset Limited.

SOOTY'S
Fireside Tales

Anna Gaffey

Age: 10

Purnell

Contents

Sooty Goes Painting

One day Sooty decided to explore up in Matthew's attic. He got very excited when he thought of all the treasure and valuable things that might be up there.

"After all," Sooty thought, "attics are always full of those sort of things, aren't they?"

In fact, he got so excited he thought he'd burst if he didn't climb up to the attic straight away.

He carefully climbed the ladder up into the roof; but he was in for a big disappointment. You see, Matthew had cleared out the attic not long ago, and it was empty except for two tins of paint.

Sooty was very upset that he didn't find any old masterpieces or interesting chests. But he was determined to do something with the two pots of paint. He thought hard for a minute.

"I know," he decided. "Matthew wanted to give the garage door a new coat of bright green paint. I'll do it for him; he *will* be surprised!"

Sooty clambered up into the attic to have a closer look at the paint. When he saw it he was even more disappointed, and it was just too much for him. He started making an awful noise, crying and blubbering! He made such a row that his friends came up the ladder to see what was the matter!

Sweep was playing downstairs with Matthew's cousins, who had come for a visit. They all rushed up to the attic to see what was the matter.

"Why are you so upset?" asked Sweep.

"I was so disappointed not to find anything exciting in the attic," sobbed Sooty. "Then I saw this paint and I thought that I would paint the garage green and give Matthew a surprise." Sniff.

"Well, that's a nice idea. Why cry about it?" said Sweep.

"Because when I got closer to the paint I saw that it wasn't green at all, only blue and yellow! I'm even more disappointed now." Sniff.

"I suppose I could paint one part of the garage blue and one part of the garage yellow," said Sooty.

Sweep thought Sooty was being very silly but, after all, it wasn't *his* great idea to explore the attic, and *he* hadn't got all excited, had he?

But Sooty's never unhappy for long. He usually has a good idea to solve most problems. Actually, this time it wasn't him who had the bright idea.

"Why don't you use some magic?" said one of Matthew's cousins. "We've heard all about it and we'd love to see you do some!"

Sooty stopped crying at once, much to Sweep's relief.

"Of course, why didn't I think of that. I'm an expert magicker, you know," he said, rather proudly.

Sooty wanted to impress his new friends with his magical powers. He stood up very importantly and carefully took his magic wand out of his pocket. Then he waved it around, a bit more than he needed to really, and in a magician's voice he said:

"Izzy-whizzy, yellows and blues,
Make a colour I can use."

But, oh dear, as usual Sooty's magic didn't go as planned. Perhaps it was because he waved his wand about too

much, but to everyone's surprise the lids popped off the paint pots and paint splashed out, spilling everywhere!

"Oh no, what a mess you've made!" said Sweep.

Sooty was very embarrassed because his magic hadn't worked in front of Matthew's guests. What an awful day he'd been having!

"Oh gosh, what will I do now?" he said. "Matthew will be very angry when he sees the mess I've made of his clean attic. I wish I'd never come up here at all! That idea of yours wasn't very good," he said to Matthew's cousin.

"I think you'd better put the paint in new pots before it runs everywhere," said Sweep.

He rushed off downstairs and quickly found an empty bucket. Sooty was so grumpy he didn't really think what he was doing. He just poured the paint quickly into the bucket to stop it from

going all over the floor. And guess what!

As everyone knows, but Sooty had forgotten, blue and yellow mixed together make green! The cousins decided Sooty was really very clever after all when they saw the paint turning a lovely bright green—and, as a matter of fact, Sooty thought he was rather clever, too! He mixed the paint properly so that there wouldn't be any streaks. Then Sooty and Sweep gave the garage a brand new bright coat of paint. Matthew was very pleased with it, and he never got to hear about the rather messy magic!

Sweep and Matthew's cousins never let on and Sooty was very grateful. He was rather embarrassed about crying, and being such a baby when things didn't go right. But he thought happily that in the end he *had* had a very interesting day—even if all the treasure in the attic *had* been cleared away!

Sooty's Magic Marrow

Sooty and Sweep like to do jobs around Matthew's house when he's out, so that he gets a nice surprise when he returns. One day he went shopping, and they knew that he would be out for quite a while. As they waved to him from the window Sooty noticed something.

"Don't the flowers look lovely in Matthew's garden," said Sooty. "Why don't we make another flower bed for him in front of the house? Then he'll be able to see the flowers from his front window."

Sooty and Sweep set to work. Sooty dug and Sweep filled his bucket with the spare earth.

But while Sooty was digging he struck water! He didn't mean to, of course. There was one piece of land which was very hard indeed. Sooty tried and tried to get his spade into it but he couldn't.

And it went in. But before Sooty had time to pull it out again there was a loud gurgling noise from under the ground and whoosh! A fountain of water shot up in the air.

And I'm afraid he got rather cross with it in the end, because he raised his spade high above his head and banged it down as hard as it would go.

"Go in!" he shouted.

Sooty could hardly believe his eyes when he saw the fountain, and he sat down and watched it soar into the sky. He felt very pleased about it really, because he had always thought that a fountain would look nice in Matthew's garden. Besides, it was nice and cool, just what Sooty and Sweep wanted!

Sooty sat and watched it for a long time and felt very happy as it sparkled up into the sky.

"Matthew will be pleased at my clever

idea," said Sooty, as though he had meant to do it all the time!

I don't think Matthew would have been very pleased though, because Sooty had broken a water pipe underground!

It was the main water supply to Matthew's house, and I think that he would rather have water in his bath than water spouting in the middle of his garden, don't you?

Sweep realised what Sooty had done when he saw the broken water pipe sticking out of the ground.

"Oh dear, now you've done it," he said.

"What a shame," said Sooty. "I did like the idea of a fountain. But I suppose I'd better mend it. What a lot of work I'm making for myself!" he sighed.

First Sooty worked some magic on the water so that it would stop coming out. Then he had to borrow Matthew's tool bag and mend the pipe as best he could.

"That gives me an idea," said Sooty. "We'd better stop gardening before we have any more accidents. We can play football instead. Matthew's cousins can join in."

"This garden is rather hard work," said Sooty.

"Perhaps I'd better dig," said Sweep. But he hit his toe with the spade and hopped around groaning!

We all have days when things don't go right, however hard we try. I'm afraid that Sooty was having one of them today. Whatever he did seemed to end in disaster, despite his best intentions. In fact, the way things went Sooty shouldn't really have got up at all that morning!

He was so pleased with his idea that he rushed off immediately to find a football in the garage, leaving Sweep still hopping around on one foot!

Oh dear! As soon as Sooty, Sweep and the cousins started to play football they had an accident which was even worse than the fountain! Sooty ran up to the ball and kicked it so hard that it soared over the house just like a bird.

Sooty looked at Sweep, and I think he was just about to bow proudly when there was a dreadful crash of breaking glass. The cousins stared solemnly at Sooty.

"You've broken the greenhouse," they said sternly.

"We'd better go and look," said Sooty sadly.

They all went round to the back of the house, and sure enough the first thing they saw when they got there was a big hole in the roof of the greenhouse.

It was quite the biggest hole Sooty had ever seen in a greenhouse, and he felt very unhappy about it. But what upset Sooty most of all was when he found the football.

Sooty knew something was the matter as soon as he saw Sweep sit down and cover his eyes with his paws.

"What's the matter, Sweep?" he asked.

Sweep raised a paw and pointed to the football, and then Sooty knew what was wrong too, because it was almost buried in Matthew's best marrow.

Of course, as soon as he saw it Sooty ran straight in and pulled the football out, but it left such a big hole in the marrow that everyone knew it would never win a prize at this afternoon's fete.

Matthew had carefully grown the marrow from a tiny plant. He had fed it very carefully and when it grew he even polished it! He was very, very proud of it, and was sure that he would win a prize for the biggest, greenest and shiniest vegetable!

You can imagine how upset he would be if he could see the horrible mess the football had made of his pride and joy.

Well, afterwards Sooty said that if they hadn't frowned the magic wouldn't have gone wrong, but I'm not too sure about that! In fact, I think Sooty must have said the wrong spell altogether, because as soon as he finished speaking, every bit of glass fell out of the greenhouse.

"Now look what you've done!" said one of the cousins.

"Your magic never works properly, Sooty," said the other.

Sweep sighed and sat down on the grass.

"Well, since you magicked the glass

There was only one thing to do. Sooty took out his wand and pointed it at the marrow.

The cousins frowned when they saw the wand. They really weren't very happy about Sooty's magic because it didn't always seem to do what he wanted.

out you had better magic it in again," he said.

Sweep was right, Sooty knew that, so he ran into the house and fetched his Book of Magic, and then he looked up the strongest spell he could find.

"Magic blow, magic grow,
Mend the greenhouse and the
marrow."

Sooty muttered the magic words to himself as he read them. And it's a good thing he did, because I don't know what would have happened if he'd said them aloud!

But as it was, there was a BANG—like a thunder-clap—and all the glass flew back into the greenhouse like lightning! The hole was mended too, but what really surprised Sooty was the way the marrow suddenly started to grow.

You've never seen anything like it in

your life! It grew fatter and fatter and fatter, until I'm sure it would have burst if Sweep hadn't run to the shops and fetched Matthew, who cut it off the stalk.

It stopped growing as soon as Matthew cut it, of course, and everyone felt very relieved. But when he saw how big it was, Matthew couldn't understand it at all, and he asked Sooty what he'd been doing.

Sooty didn't tell him, though; he just smiled very sweetly and asked if he could help to carry the marrow to the car.

Well, Sooty had to tell him, of course, because it really *was* rather odd! Matthew was very surprised, but he wasn't too angry because Sooty had repaired all the damage he had done.

The marrow was so big that they could hardly lift it!

They had an awful job getting it through the greenhouse door, too, and it wouldn't go inside the car at all. So Sooty and Sweep had to sit on the roof and hold it at each end, while Matthew's cousins leaned out of the windows and held each side.

Of course, it won the First Prize easily when they got to the fete because it was quite the biggest marrow in the show. Sooty said it must be the biggest marrow in the world.

But Sooty cheated just a little bit, didn't he?

Sooty Buys a Car

One day Sooty decided to buy a car. He saw a nice blue one, and because it was the cheapest car he'd ever seen he bought it.

The salesman put the money in his pocket and ran off down the road so quickly that Sooty didn't even have time to say goodbye! But he didn't mind because he was busy climbing into his little car.

Sooty blew the horn and then he pushed all the knobs, but it didn't start. He felt a bit worried as he climbed out again and lifted the bonnet, and he was beginning to wonder if the salesman had cheated him.

Anyway, the engine looked all right, although Sooty wouldn't have known if it didn't.

He was just going to put the bonnet down again when he saw a slot marked '2p'. Well, of course, as soon as Sooty

saw that he knew what to do, because he'd seen lots of cars like this at fairs and seasides.

It was lucky he'd got 2p in his pocket. He put it in the slot and jumped into his little car, and before you could say "speed limit" it was roaring down the road like a racing car. Sooty had a wonderful time driving along the road and everybody waved at him as he went by.

The trouble started when Sooty drove up the High Street. You see, a policeman was directing the traffic and he was holding his arm up. So, of course, Sooty would have stopped if he could.

But he didn't know how to, and that

must have frightened him a bit because he just drove straight at the policeman as he stood in the middle of the street!

The policeman could hardly believe his eyes, and I'm sure that if the 2p in Sooty's car hadn't run out just at that moment Sooty would have knocked him over. But fortunately it did, so Sooty's car only dented the buttons on his tunic a tiny bit.

Sooty got out of the car. He hadn't got 2p so he couldn't make it go.

"I'll magic it," he said.

But he was much too flustered to think of a spell properly, and the one he tried didn't work. All the cars in the High Street stopped going, and everyone was very cross.

Sooty was so embarrassed that he looked down shamefully at the road. And guess what? He saw a 2p piece lying on the pavement!

Just as Sooty was about to pick it up the Mayor of the town came along and spoke to Sooty in a very concerned voice.

"Excuse me, Sooty, but that's my 2p. I dropped it just now and I've come back looking for it."

By this time Sooty was a bit tired of his new car.

"Well, since my car goes on 2p's you

may as well use it," he said to the Mayor.

The Mayor was very pleased, as he had got quite tired looking for his 2p and fancied a ride back to the Council offices.

He got in and Sooty waved his magic wand to make all the cars go again. This time the magic worked!

It worked so well that the little car sped off so fast that the Mayor didn't quite know what to do! He probably got the hang of it, though. And I think Sooty's safer walking on the pavement, don't you?

Sooty at the Zoo

It was Sweep's birthday, and for a treat he and Sooty were going to the Zoo. Sooty was very excited about it, because he'd never been to the Zoo before.

They bought their tickets at the gate and walked into the Zoo, and they had a lovely time looking at all the animals.

The Keeper said they could watch all the lions being fed if they liked, and Sooty was very pleased because he was allowed to carry the bucket of meat.

Sooty thought the lions were beautiful, but the one he liked best of all was the big, old lion who lived in a cage by himself.

The Keeper said he would feed the old lion first, and they were just walking over to his cage when the wind blew the Keeper's hat off.

The hat bowled along the ground and sailed straight through the bars into the lion's cage.

"Bother!" said the Keeper crossly. "Now I've lost my hat."

"No, you haven't," said Sooty, proudly taking out his wand. "I'll magic it out for you."

The Keeper looked quite pleased when Sooty said that—but then, he didn't know Sooty's magic like we do, did he? Anyway, Sooty muttered some magic words and waved his wand, and then he waited for the spell to work. And it did . . . in a way!

But, of course, Sooty really meant the hat to come to the Keeper, so he was very surprised when the Keeper went to the hat instead!

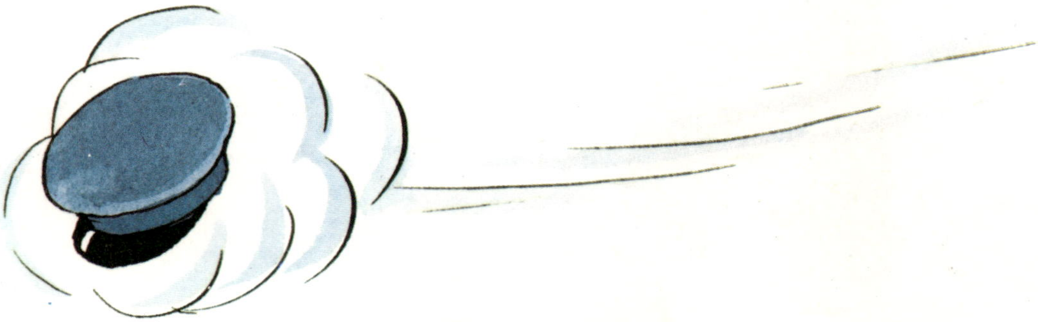

He just rose in the air and sailed through the bars into the lion's cage. It must have squashed him a bit, too, but he didn't really notice, because he thought the lion was going to eat him.

I expect it would have done, too, if he'd stayed in the cage very long, but he ran straight to the door and shouted to Sooty.

"Let me out!"

Now Sooty was dreadfully sorry that he'd magicked the Keeper into the lion's cage, so he ran straight over and opened the door to let him out.

Sooty wasn't to know that the lion would jump out as well, was he? But, anyway, that's what happened. And do you know, it chased the Keeper all round the Zoo!

Although the Keeper had looked after the lion for a long time, and fed and talked to him every day, it was a different matter when the lion was outside the cage. The Keeper didn't feel like talking at all; he felt like running away!

He *was* in a state, and he kept shouting

at Sooty to do something about the lion.

Well, Sooty did try, but when the lion turned and looked at him Sooty didn't really like to argue with him. And when the lion growled at him he climbed up a tree so fast he didn't even have time to put the bucket of food down, so he took it with him.

Sooty was very relieved when the lion started chasing the Keeper again, although he didn't really have time to make himself comfortable in the tree before the Keeper came running round the corner.

"Drop the bucket!" shouted the Keeper, as he ran towards the tree. Sooty dropped the bucket like a stone, which was rather a shame, because it fell right on the Keeper's head!

The Keeper sat down under the tree with stars shooting around his head, and all the meat spilled on the ground. It's a good thing it did, too, because the lion stopped and ate the meat instead of the Keeper.

Sooty didn't know what to do. He sat up in the tree and hoped that the lion would soon be full-up and wouldn't feel like eating any little bears.

The lion certainly seemed to enjoy his meal. It was because he was being so greedy that Sweep managed to sneak up on him secretly.

Sweep had run straight off to fetch a net when he saw the Keeper in the cage. He threw it over the lion like lightning, and Sooty climbed down the tree and helped Sweep tie up the lion.

Then they took the bucket off the Keeper's head. They thought he would be very pleased when he saw they'd caught the lion, but he wasn't! Sooty was a bit hurt about it. Because, after all, he had saved the Keeper's life, hadn't he?

The Mystery Mansion Adventure

It was Sooty's birthday! When Sooty and Sweep got up in the morning there were presents scattered all over the living-room floor.

They were soon busy looking through the pile of exciting things. There were books and paints, a carpenter's set, a tin of toffee and a cowboy's outfit, a penknife—in fact, so many things that Sooty and Sweep didn't know where to look first!

But Sooty couldn't help thinking that he liked his present from Matthew, a beautiful bouncy red ball, best of all.

Sooty wanted to play with the ball straight away, but Sweep said that it might break a window or knock over a vase, and perhaps they had better play with one of the safer toys.

Sooty was a bit disappointed, but Sweep made a sensible suggestion:

"Why don't we go outside and play with the ball? As long as we don't break the glass in the greenhouse or spoil the flowers, Matthew won't mind at all."

Sooty thought that this was a very good idea. They went out into the garden and just then a little Clown came along. He lived with the circus which had come to town; but he didn't know anyone to play with and he was rather bored. When he saw Sooty and Sweep playing with the ball he asked if he could join in.

Sooty and Sweep were having a wonderful time throwing and catching the ball. But when the little Clown caught the ball and joined in, he threw it quite hard and Sooty was taken by surprise.

He couldn't catch it and he fell back, right into Matthew's tulips! Several flowers were broken.

"Oh dear," said Sooty. "You *can* come and play with us, little Clown; but we'd better find somewhere a bit more open!"

Sooty and Sweep liked their new friend, even if he was a bit clumsy with Sooty's new ball. He was dressed in a blue clown suit and he had a big yellow bell on the front of it. He wore a hat with an orange bobble, and he had clown make up on his face.

"I think we're going to have fun today!" said Sooty, and he didn't know how right he was!

It was a lovely sunny day and the three friends set off for a nearby field. Sooty held the ball tightly, in case he dropped it and it got lost.

They soon found the very spot for their game. Sooty even found a strong, flat piece of wood which had been hanging loose on a fence; it was just the right shape for a rounders bat.

"We'll take it in turns to field," said Sooty. "Sweep can do it first, while I throw the ball and the little Clown hits it." They went right out into the middle of the field, so that they wouldn't hit anything.

Sooty threw the ball and the little Clown was so clever at hitting it with the piece of wood that it went right over the fence into someone's allotment! Sweep was so long finding it among the cabbages that he was quite cross when he came back to them.

"Let me hit now," he asked Sooty. "You throw and the little Clown can field. I've had my turn!"

"All right," said Sooty, though the little Clown didn't look very pleased at this idea.

He grumpily walked to the edge of the field to catch Sooty's hit.

When Sooty threw the ball to Sweep, he hit it so hard that the little Clown had to run all the way to the level crossing before he found it, and he was very cross indeed when he got back.

"I'm tired of this game," he grumbled.

"Let's see how high we can throw the ball," said Sooty. "The one who throws the highest of all can choose the next game."

"Oh yes," replied his friends. "That's a wonderful idea, Sooty!"

"Unless you do the fetching part, Sooty, I'd rather play something else."

Sooty did not want to do the fetching either, so he and Sweep agreed with the little Clown that it was time to try another game.

Sweep began the game by pointing to a tall elm and saying:

"I can throw the ball higher than that tree. You watch!"

He picked up the ball and threw it up and, sure enough, it rose as high as the

The Disappearing Ball

elm. Some rooks sitting in their nests squawked in surprise when the ball whizzed past them.

Catching the ball neatly, the little Clown said:

"Phoo, that's nothing. Watch ME! I can throw it right over that telegraph pole—up one side and down the other!"

He threw the ball and it rose up and up and up, and did just what the little Clown said it would do.

It went up above the tree, and then it sailed down again and they chased after it.

"Oh dear," said Sooty. "I wish I hadn't boasted about my throwing. I never *really* thought that I was *that* good, I really didn't!"

After a while Sooty and his friends realised that the ball really *was* lost in the sky, unless it had come down somewhere a long way away—or had landed on the Moon!

Now Sooty knew that he would have to be very clever indeed to beat the little Clown and Sweep at this game—they were so good at it.

"Well, I can throw so high that it won't come down at all," he boasted. "Do you want to see me?"

The friends nodded their heads. They didn't believe that even Sooty could be *that* clever!

He took the ball and threw it up and up—in fact the ball kept on going up. The three friends watched it until they couldn't see it any more, then they became rather worried. Supposing Sooty was really as clever as he said he was! What would Matthew say when Sooty lost his new birthday present?

They waited and waited, staring up at the sky until their eyes hurt.

He looked up to see a bird beckoning to him with its wing. Sooty went up as close to the bird as he could, because he knew that the bird would be too shy and nervous to fly down to him.

They were just deciding to go home and own up to Matthew that they had lost Sooty's present, when Sooty heard a "Coo-ee!" sound coming from a nearby tree.

"Hello, did you want me?" said Sooty.

"Yes," answered the bird. "I saw your ball fly right over the garden wall of Mystery Mansion."

"Oh, thank you!" said Sooty gratefully. "I was feeling rather worried about that ball. I'll just pop over now and get it."

"Mind how you go!" warned the bird, but Sooty had already gone to fetch his friends to tell them what he was going to do.

The three ran towards Mystery Mansion. They knew where it was because it was the biggest house for miles. There was a high wall all round it, and after looking at it very carefully Sooty realised that it was going to be very difficult to climb over the top.

"How do you get in, Sooty?" asked the little Clown.

Sooty's usually very good at finding ways of doing difficult things, and the two friends were sure that he'd solve this problem without any trouble.

"I'll have to have a think," said Sooty. "You two sit quietly until I've finished."

Sweep and the little Clown stayed very still and waited for Sooty to get an idea for climbing high walls. They didn't have to wait very long!

"I've got it!" said Sooty, jumping up. "We'll climb on each other's backs like the acrobats do at the circus! Sweep, you stand close by the wall."

Sweep did as he was told.

"Now, little Clown, you climb on top of Sweep and stand on his back."

The little Clown did as *he* was told, though it was rather difficult as they all had to keep stopping to have a good laugh at themselves; then Sweep would wiggle and the little Clown would fall off!

However, the little Clown got safely balanced at last, and Sooty, being the clever one, climbed up his friends quite easily. When he stood on the little Clown's shoulders he was able to reach the top of the wall without any trouble at all.

"You'd better wait here," said Sooty. "I'll be as quick as I can."

The Big House was very large and rather frightening. It had a big wooden door and lots of barred windows of different shapes and sizes. There were lots of different rooftops and towers. One tower was round, with a large weather-vane on the top, in the shape of a cockerel. It swung around as the wind blew it. That was the only sign of movement. There was no one playing in the garden or looking out of the windows.

Sooty had never seen the house properly before, and he was quite scared because it looked so dark and mysterious. He stood looking at it for quite a while and then said: "Right, I'd better go in . . ."

Sooty's friends didn't say anything—they were too puffed out with Sooty's weight on them to speak properly! So Sooty stood on top of the wall and jumped down safely on the other side, landing in a bed of Forget-me-nots.

Looking wasn't as easy as he'd thought, because the ground was covered in leaves. There were lots of garden beds full of pretty flowers. The ball could be anywhere!

He was just wondering if the bird could have made a mistake about the ball, when there, just a little way in front of him, but hiding under a large leaf, was something that looked just like it!

Good! Now he was in the garden at last, and he only had to find the ball, then they could all go home to tea. He started to creep about quietly (in case there were any unfriendly people about), looking closely at everything that was round and shiny.

Sooty ran up to the big leaf to pick up

Trapped in Mystery Mansion!

what he thought was the precious ball—but dear, oh dear, it wasn't a ball at all but a big red apple! He had picked it up before he saw what a silly mistake he had made.

Perhaps, after all, he had better get the other two to help him look for the ball. The garden really WAS enormous, far too big for a small bear to search thoroughly all by himself.

He ran back to the wall and called softly:

"Sweep! Little Clown! Are you still there?"

"Of course we are!" replied Sweep. "Have you found it yet?"

"Not quite," answered Sooty. "I think you two had better come and help me look."

"How can we get over the wall without you?" asked Sweep.

Now Sooty hadn't thought of that, but he said:

"I'm just going to have another think! Don't worry, I'll be as quick as I can getting you over."

He sat on a big stone to have a think, and as he did so he happened to see a shed not far away from where he was sitting.

"A ladder!" he said to himself. "There's sure to be a ladder somewhere, perhaps there's one in that shed!"

In no time at all he was inside the shed. Yes—there was the very thing he wanted!

He crept quietly into the shed, in case there was anyone in there. Then he carried the ladder out under his arm.

He dragged it up to the Forget-me-not bed and propped it up against the wall. From the top of the ladder Sooty stood on the wall, pulled the ladder up after him and told his friends to lift it over.

"Make sure you fix it firmly on your side," said Sooty. "And the last one up must pull it over the wall into the garden again."

"You are clever to think of that, Sooty," said both his friends, as they did what he told them. They managed to get the ladder back into the garden quite safely, and Sooty hid it under some bushes.

"We'll need it when we leave," he explained cleverly to the others.

"Sooty, you think of *everything*!" they both exclaimed.

Sooty could not help feeling that he WAS rather clever but did not stop to say so just then.

"Come on, we *must* find that ball before someone comes out of the house and finds US," he said. "I'll look over there under the holly bushes and you two go over by the garden seat. The first to see the ball can give a whistle."

The three ran off quietly, looking

carefully under leaves and twigs and even behind stones, but they could not see anything that was the tiniest bit like the ball.

Just as Sooty was crawling out of a privet hedge where he thought the ball might be hidden, he heard angry shouts and terrified squeaks. Quickly he ran towards the sounds and was horrified to see Sweep and the little Clown being dragged along one on each side of a very fierce man!

"Oh, my goodness! What do we do now?" Sooty asked himself. "I daren't stop to have a think!"

So, instead, he followed the three

figures, keeping very quiet and out of sight among the bushes and shrubs. He watched the man take Sweep and the little Clown into the house and shut the door behind him.

'Idea for Getting People Out of Strange Houses', and he would do that better if he wasn't shut up himself.

Sooty hid behind a tree and was just sitting down to think again, when he

Sooty wasn't afraid that the man would come out for *him*, because he knew that his friends would not let anyone know that he was there at all. They would be relying on him to find an

happened to peep round the tree trunk and see the man come out of the house again, followed by another older man who had no hair at all on his head.

They locked the front door behind

them, then left the garden by a strong wooden door which Sooty could hear being locked on the outside.

Sooty decided that he would risk creeping up to the house to see if he could see any sign of his friends. Of course, there might be more fierce men about, he thought, so it would be best to be very careful.

He reached Mystery Mansion safely, and going up close to the wall of the house, gave a whistle, which sounded

just like a robin twittering. Almost at once he heard another robin-like sound—it was Sweep answering. The sound came from right above Sooty's head.

He looked up and there, behind a barred window, were the faces of the two little prisoners.

High above his head he saw Sweep and the little Clown, looking out of a barred window. They had been locked in by the man who had caught them, and he had taken the key away.

Sooty didn't think it was safe to call to them, so he made signs showing them that he was going to explore round the house and find a way in, somehow.

He saw their faces begin to smile so he knew they understood what he was going to do and were feeling more cheerful.

He could see at once that the window of their room was much too high to reach with the ladder, so he began to look around for another way of getting inside Mystery Mansion.

On the other side of the house he saw just what he wanted—a good branchy tree growing quite near to the side of the house and, not too far up, an open window!

"I'll be inside in a jiffy!" he thought happily, as he began to climb the tree.

As he climbed the tree Sooty wondered why his friends had been locked in.

"There must be something very strange going on in this old house," he said to himself. "Perhaps a Robber gang lives here!" He got quite excited and forgot to be frightened!

Sooty's Exciting Discovery

Sooty found the tree a very easy one to climb. In no time at all he was at the top. When he looked around him, though, he had a terrible disappointment, for he found that he could not reach the window after all—it was quite a long way away. What was he going to do now?

While Sooty sat on the top of the tree waiting for an idea to come—suddenly one DID come and it was such a simple idea that Sooty nearly fell out of the tree with surprise.

His magic wand, of course! There was still a little magic in it, just about enough to magic this tree for him, he felt sure.

So he took the wand out of its secret hiding place in his pocket and tapped the top branch of the tree. He tapped until the wand was empty.

Gradually the branch began to grow and grow, and very soon Sooty was able to climb along it and through the open window of the house. At last he was in Mystery Mansion—Sweep and the little Clown were as good as rescued already!

Very, very carefully he tiptoed up to each door upstairs until he heard Sweep's bird whistle. It came from the other side of a door which had a key in the outside lock.

Wasn't that lucky? Sooty did not need to be very clever to open it at once and let out the prisoners. And were they glad to see him! They shook his paws and patted him on the back and told him how clever he was.

"Don't mention it," Sooty replied modestly!

"Let's have a look round, shall we?" he whispered. "There doesn't seem to be anyone about and we might find some hidden treasure or a secret passage or something really mysterious like that."

Sweep and the little Clown agreed at once. They each went in a different direction, just like real detectives, opening doors and cupboards very quietly, in case anything jumped out of them. Suddenly Sweep and the little Clown heard Sooty call them in an excited voice.

"Come here, boys!" he cried. "I've found something really peculiar—it's what they call a lab—lab—YOU know, a place where grown-ups play with real chemistry sets until they invent something new. Look at all the bottles and tubes and things!"

It really *was* a laboratory, just as Sooty had said. It looked very mysterious, too, for the windows had bars across them; there were dark shutters for keeping it private at night, and on the door was a notice that said:

'VERY PRIVATE. KEEP OUT.
DANGER.
NO TRESPASSERS ALLOWED.'

"Anyone would think they wanted to keep the place to themselves!" said the little Clown.

"How silly! Let's have a look round," said Sooty.

"Yes, let's!" replied Sooty. "You two explore while I try to make some magic. I'd like to fill up my wand if I can; I've used a lot of its magic today."

While his friends were busy picking up bottles and opening tins, Sooty chose a few coloured liquids and started to stir them in a bowl with a wooden spoon. How pretty the colours were!

The liquids did not smell a bit nice, but Sooty did not mind that as long as they turned into magic.

He stirred harder and harder, but nothing much seemed to happen, so he put the mixture that he'd made into an empty jar and started again with the most interesting bottles he could find on the shelves. There were all sorts of shapes: tall ones, short ones, fat ones and thin ones.

"I like being an inventor!" said Sooty. Actually he was rather a messy inventor.

VERY PRIVATE.
KEEP OUT!
DANGER
NO TRESPASSERS ALLOWED.

He spilt quite a lot of the different mixtures, and they ran down the table onto the floor. He made quite a lot of coloured smoke, too. He really *was* enjoying himself!

Sooty had just made a beautiful blue liquid, and it was just beginning to bubble nicely when they all heard voices from below. They had been so interested in what they were doing that they had not heard the front door open downstairs.

the floor with a crash.

That did it! Up the stairs ran the two men, the young man first and the Old Gentleman panting up after him. Sooty and Sweep and the little Clown rushed

"Golly!" said Sooty. "We're discovered!"

He was so scared that he upset the bubbling blue liquid, and they were all three splashed with it. The glass fell to

out of the laboratory door and up the next flight of stairs.

"After them!" called the Old Gentleman to the young one. "They mustn't get away. They might have discovered something!"

The three friends were up the stairs, into an attic and through the window onto the roof in a flash. Once on the roof they knew that they were saved, for the tree that Sooty had magicked had grown higher than the house by now, and it was easy for them to jump on one of its branches and so get away safely—or so they thought . . .

But as Sooty, Sweep and the little Clown climbed onto the tree, they were horrified to see the young man climb up after them. (They had forgotten that sometimes grown-ups like climbing trees, too!)

The man had almost got hold of Sweep's tail when Sooty shouted to his pals:

"There's only one thing we *can* do now—jump! If that man doesn't catch us in the tree he'll catch us in the garden! So let's go—one, two, three, JUMP!"

As they said "JUMP", the three friends shut their eyes and jumped, hoping to goodness that they would land on something soft.

And DID they land on something soft?

They did NOT. In fact they didn't land at all—they FLEW! As they flew through the air like birds their eyes opened wide in astonishment.

"Yes, Sooty," replied his friends very politely. "You really are clever!"

Although Sooty felt that they were right, he didn't want to seem vain so he didn't say anything. But they were all happy and glad that all they had to do now was to fly, like birds, all the way home.

As for the two men, *they* were so surprised that they could only stare and stare.

"There must have been some magic left in your wand after all, Sooty!" gasped the little Clown.

"Unless you made some flying magic by mistake," panted Sweep. "Some of that blue stuff spilled on us, remember."

"You may be right, Sweep. I don't know *what* I made," replied Sooty. "But it must have been something very special. What a good thing you had me with you today!"

A Sort of Rescue

As they flew merrily along, Sooty began to think about tea, and his tummy began to rumble.

"Sooty, it's thundering!" cried Sweep, his ears pricking up with alarm. "Let's go down now before the storm starts!"

"Don't be silly, Sweep!" said Sooty. "It's only my tummy asking me when I'm going to send down some tea!"

"Well, when ARE you, Sooty? Going to send down some tea, I mean!" replied the little Clown. "I'm hungry, too. Let's all have tea now."

"I'd like to," said Sooty. "But I don't

know how to go down, as a matter of fact."

"But . . . Sooty!" shouted his friends. "You *must* know!"

"I'm afraid I didn't get that far with my magic," said Sooty.

"We thought you knew absolutely *everything*! Can't you think of an idea?"

"How can I, silly!" replied Sooty crossly. "I can't get ideas unless I'm sitting down, you know that." There was no answer to this, so the three flew on glumly, not bothering to look where they were going.

Once Sweep flew right into a bird carrying a beakful of fur to its new nest, and it dropped the lot. Later the little Clown bumped into a television aerial

and the people viewing below looked at the back of their set to see what had gone wrong.

By now they had flown so far that they were almost over a local Sweet Factory, with its tall chimney sticking right up into the sky.

Suddenly Sweep called:

"Sooty, look out! There's a factory chimney right in front of you—be careful!"

"We're much too high to bump into that," replied Sooty, but as he spoke he noticed that all three of them were not nearly so high in the sky as they had been.

In fact, they were getting lower and lower every minute.

"I think my flying magic is nearly used up," he called to the others.

"So's mine!" cried the little Clown, looking scared.

"And mine!" cried Sweep. "We're falling fast!"

Indeed, just as they came over the top of the chimney, they DID fall, one by one, right inside the chimney into the factory below.

Oh dear! They picked themselves up,

gave themselves a good shake and looked around feeling a bit dazed.

"We'll soon be out of here," boasted Sooty to his friends, who were looking at him as if the whole adventure were

a thing used in sweet factories for carrying the sweets through different parts of the factory where they are covered with chocolate, then with paper, ready to send to the shops.

his fault. "Just leave it to me!"

At that moment he saw what looked like a long shelf moving along smoothly from one side to the other. It was what grown-ups call a conveyor-belt, which is

"It's a railway leading out of the factory," said Sooty, hoping that his guess was right. "Let's get on it—quickly, follow me, everyone!"

They climbed on to the belt, one

behind the other, and it carried them along at a fine speed.

In no time at all they were not outside, as Sooty had hoped, but in the part of the factory where the sweets were covered in chocolate. Before they knew what was happening, a big thing like a funnel was pouring milk chocolate over them, covering them all over.

While they still gulped and gasped, their mouths full of chocolate, the belt took them along to the next part of the factory, where another wonderful machine wrapped them up, first in silver paper and then in coloured paper—pink for Sooty, blue for Sweep and green for the little Clown.

By now they were all so puzzled and flustered that no good ideas could come to any of them!

Sooty couldn't make out what was happening. It all seemed very mysterious to the three friends.

Looking like very unusual parcels, they were carried by the belt into the end part of the factory, where the sweets were sorted out ready to be sent to the shops.

Now this was a very fussy factory; only the nicest possible sweets were allowed to go from it to the shops. Any that looked a bit odd or peculiar were put in a heap by themselves.

The man who looked after this part of the factory stared hard at the three strange packages.

"No-one would want to buy *these* sweets!" he thought, and took them off the conveyor-belt.

The only idea that Sooty had was to shout: "Help!"

It worked because it really made the man jump and he quickly unwrapped the parcels. He was very angry with the three friends for wasting all the chocolate and paper, and when they said that they had accidentally flown down the chimney he wouldn't believe them and he called a policeman!

Sooty's Reward

The policeman decided that Sooty, Sweep and the little Clown were *very* suspicious characters. He thought that they'd broken into the Sweet Factory to steal the chocolate. When they told him about their flying adventure he frowned and said:

"Right, that's enough tale-telling. Since you're being so cheeky I'm going to take you to the station, and I'd like to see you fly out of there!"

They all went to the Police Station. Sooty was very worried and had run out of ideas altogether. His friends didn't say anything—they didn't like the idea of being locked up twice in one day, and this time there would be no key in the door to help them escape.

When they arrived at the Police Station they had another shock. For sitting there waiting for them was the Old Gentleman from Mystery Mansion! But what most surprised them was that he didn't seem angry at all. In fact, he seemed overjoyed to see them!

when I saw you flying away from my house this afternoon that you had found the secret of making flying magic—the secret I have been trying to find for fifty years!"

"Don't look so worried all of you!" he called gaily. "I'm delighted to see you again! When you played with the things in my laboratory I ended up as pleased as a dog with two tails! You see, I knew

He patted their heads kindly and tickled Sweep behind the ears.

"Now you're coming back to my house to show me how you did it!"

At this Sooty got really worried.

Whatever could he do? After all, he had made the flying magic quite by accident and he could not possibly do it again, he was sure.

But if he told the Old Gentleman that, they might be put in prison after all. So he just said:

"I'll do my best, Sir."

Sooty hoped that perhaps an idea would come into his head just in time to save them—after all, it had happened before!

There was a car outside the Police Station, with the young man from Mystery Mansion in the driving seat. The Old Gentleman told Sooty and his friends to get in the back and he climbed in after them.

As they were driven off, Sooty tried hard to get a helpful idea, but he was so sleepy and hungry that his head could only get thoughts about bed and supper, which was no good at all.

The three were fast asleep by the time

they arrived at Mystery Mansion. "Wake up, Sleepy Heads!" they heard as they were shaken gently. "Come along to the laboratory—I can't wait to see how the flying magic is made!"

They went sleepily up the stairs and into the laboratory, where a fresh supply of coloured liquids and a clean bowl were waiting for Sooty.

"Take your time," said the Old Gentleman. "Sit here beside me and I will take notes of everything you do. You others watch over there."

Sooty sat down obediently. He tried to remember what he had done earlier in the day to make the flying magic. But it was no good.

Hours and hours later he was still

mixing up the coloured liquids, but no magic had appeared. By then Sweep and the little Clown were snoring on the floor, and the young man was dozing and yawning on a nearby chair.

The Old Gentleman was feeling a bit fidgety himself, but did not stop making notes for one minute.

Sooty's hands had become so shaky

and his eyes so full of sleep that he just worked on without even seeing what he was doing.

So he was even more surprised than the Old Gentleman when the mixture in the bowl began to bubble and froth and sizzle in a most astonishing way. It was all the colours of the rainbow and had a really horrid smell.

The Old Gentleman was so thrilled at this that he put his face right up to the bowl to get a better look, and the stuff inside splashed all over his head and chin. He did not seem to mind this at all but kept on writing as fast as he could.

Suddenly he was interrupted by Sooty. "Quick! Oh *look* at your head—and your chin!" he cried.

The young man was wide awake now; even Sweep and the little Clown had opened their eyes and were blinking in amazement. For the Old Gentleman's head was covered by beautiful golden curls—he had a curly moustache and a beard that reminded Sooty of Father Christmas.

The young man had fetched a mirror and was holding it up to his master's face.

"See for yourself, Sir!" he exclaimed. "See for yourself!"

What he saw in the mirror so surprised the Old Gentleman that at first he could not say a word. Then he turned to Sooty and shook his paw.

He patted Sooty's back until the little bear nearly fell over.

"Sooty! How very clever you are!"

Sooty blushed at this because he knew he hadn't really been clever at all this time.

"Why—this magic hair grower is *much* more valuable than flying magic! I'll be able to make it and sell it to millions of people and earn heaps of money in no time! I must reward you—would £5 do?"

"Gosh, thank you," replied Sooty, still feeling rather dizzy. "But first, please may we have something to eat? We haven't had anything since lunch —except chocolate."

The Old Gentleman was really excited about having hair again after so many years. He kept on stroking his head and looking in the mirror. Sooty couldn't really understand it because, of course, he's always been furry all over!

"I'm sorry that I didn't make the flying spell," he said. "I'm afraid I can't remember what was in it. Perhaps when I have some tea I'll remember."

"Never mind, never mind," said the Old Gentleman. "It would have been a bit dangerous anyway, what with people flying about, bumping into each other and dropping down chimneys. This hair tonic is much more harmless."

By this time Sweep was really hungry.

"I wonder whether I could have a biscuit," he said politely.

"Of course, of course," was the eager reply. "Let's go down to the kitchen and see what there is in the larder."

Very soon Sooty, Sweep and the little Clown were enjoying the most delicious supper they had ever had. They ate sausages, chips, trifle and sugar biscuits and drank ginger beer and milk. They had so much that when they tried to stand up they nearly toppled over!

"Dear, dear!" laughed the Old Gentleman (who now looked quite new). "We had better take you home in the car—you'll *never* walk there, I can see!"

"Remind me to buy a brush and comb tomorrow," he added, proudly patting his curls.

The three friends had to be practically lifted into the car, they were so full and so tired, but Sooty remembered to say "Thank you" for the reward, which was tucked safely in his pocket with his magic wand.

They were just saying goodbye when the young man held out something to Sooty.

"Is this yours, by any chance?" he asked. "I found it in the garden this afternoon."

It was the lost ball! Sooty took it joyfully. "Oh, *thank* you!" he said. "It's exactly what we wanted to make our Mystery Mansion adventure end happily!"